Then & Now

MARGATE

The Camera Obscura on the jetty, which gave a 360-degree panorama of the coast projected by lenses on to a flat screen.

A coaster safely grounded on the sands. Many were wrecked on the nearby rocks during winter storms.

Then & Now
MARGATE

Compiled by
Alan and Ian Kay

TEMPUS

Tempus Publishing Limited
The Mill, Brimscombe Port,
Stroud, Gloucestershire, GL5 2QG

ISBN 0 7524 1148 9

Typesetting and origination by
Tempus Publishing Limited
Printed in Great Britain by
Midway Clark Printing, Wiltshire

Bathing fashion around seventy-five years ago.

Contents

In 1910 there were thirty-five licensed bath chair attendants in Margate. Happily modern medical advances have eliminated the need for this type of recuperation.

Then & Now:
Visual Changes

Views from the seaside resort of Margate provide visual evidence of how it used to be in the days of our parents and grandparents. The comparison between contemporary scenes and activities provide warm, nostalgic memories for older residents to savour, while younger inhabitants and newcomers to the town will be encouraged to enquire and speculate as to the reasons for the changes.

Margate is recorded as being this country's first commercial sea bathing resort in 1736. As a traditional seaside town it has experienced many changes through the years. Social and economic changes have influenced what present-day visitors demand from their holidays. Seaside resorts like Margate now face increasing competition from the exotic locations with more attractive climates featured in the colourful brochures of the travel agents.

This collection of visual memories endeavours to compare many of these changes by showing a scene of Margate's past with, wherever possible, a photograph taken from the same angle at the present time. Some scenes from the past obviously cannot always have a contemporary comparison. The Edwardian photograph shown opposite, an invalid in a bath chair on Margate promenade, has no modern comparison as few visitors today visit the town for medical reasons.

Change occurs in many forms. Illustrations vary from the ravages of winter storms and coastal erosion to the changes in the functions of individual buildings and streets as the patterns of holidaymaking change. There are contrasts between years of neglect and the brash 'Golden Mile' of computerized electronic games and the flashing neon signs of the space age amusement arcades.

The greatest asset of Margate is its nine miles of golden sands, where once again comparisons are made between Then and Now. The concert parties, the bathing machines and the Punch and Judy have now given way to trampolining, jet skis and bouncy castles. The great indiscriminate pre-war mass of 'London by the Sea' with its cheerful Cockney jollity and vulgarity has now been replaced by family groups quietly relaxing in deck chairs with children enjoying more organized activities. Open-air bathing in the cold waters of the sea and bathing pools seems to have given way to the temperature-controlled indoor pool of the Hartsdown Leisure Centre.

History is not only about changes in buildings and streets but it is also about people. Some pages show how fashions in clothing have changed through the years. Casual holiday clothing only seems to have made its appearance in post-war years. Earlier photographs show that visitors came on holiday in their normal working clothes. Hats, suits, collars and ties preceded the present fashion of sweat shirts and jeans. Contrasts in bathing fashions are even more marked, with any exposed flesh between neck and knees covered in enveloping material.

Another change is the demise of the great luxury hotels which encouraged the development of Cliftonville in the late nineteenth century. These hotels have now been demolished and replaced by buildings catering for Margate's new type of visitor. A typical example is the site of the once elegant 300-room Cliftonville Hotel now occupied by a bowling alley and night club. The present 'classless' type of visitor no longer demands the lavish luxury amenities once supplied by the local pool of servile labour now so difficult to obtain.

The development of any seaside resort also depends to a great extent on transport facilities. Margate offers many examples of these changes. The first visitors came by sea. The sailing hoys were followed by the steam packets and paddle steamers, to be met at the harbour by the horse brakes. This was followed in turn by the railway age, the visitors making use of the tramway system and charabancs. The traditional fortnight's 'bucket and spade' holiday for Londoners is gradually being replaced by shorter stays using the town as a touring base for other Kent attractions and day trips to the Continent.

It is hoped that readers will enjoy these selective contrasts between the 'Then and Now' of a typical British seaside resort. Margate has catered for holidays from 1736 to the present day, changing through the years as events and people have changed.

Margate, like many other seaside resorts, is now undergoing a renaissance with many imaginative projects in the planning stage. It is to be hoped these progressive schemes will revitalize the resort as it enters the twenty-first century.

Visual evidence provided by postcards and photographs from the past allow us to preserve and contemplate those days when life had a gentler pace. Thus the process of visual comparison between Then and Now will be available as a nudge to memory for future generations.

The obituary of seaside resorts such as Margate has yet to be written.

One
More Visitors,
Resort Expansion

In 1929 Margate General Hospital opened amid open cornfields. Now many acres are covered by the numerous medical departments of the newly opened Queen Mother Hospital.

The building of promenades opened up previously underdeveloped areas of the town. Minnis Bay, Birchington, was developed at the turn of the century as an exclusive estate for wealthy London residents.

Today it is completely developed with an attractive bungalow estate where the retired bring their pensions and their memories. A high rise block of flats has replaced the Minnis Bay Hotel which was built in 1905.

Marine Terrace was originally built as a terrace of early Victorian apartment houses, some of the most elegant and graceful in the town. They would be rented for the whole summer season by Londoners who would bring down their own servants and carriages.

Between the wars the ground floors were converted into restaurants and souvenir shops. Today amusement arcades, bingo parlours, rock stalls and snack bars attract the day trippers. It is now the 'Golden Mile' of neon-signed colour and strident noise.

With the expansion of Margate as a popular holiday resort, roads leading into the town had to change from country lanes suitable for horses and carts into wider highways maintained to modern standards.

The growth of private car ownership and coach travel meant the village pond shown above had to be cleared. The road traffic is seasonal in nature, but several schemes have been projected for providing a bypass.

The Harbour & Lighthouse, Margate.

Margate has had a harbour since the thirteenth century. The pre-war scene was lively, with a small fishing industry, pleasure boats and Thames barges bringing in bricks, timber and ballast. Colliers from the north east would berth with gas coal for the local gasworks.

Today the harbour is quiet and relatively unused. Silting has meant that coasters can no longer enter, the gasworks have closed and heavy materials now come to the town by road and rail.

14

Before the Second World War, the harbour area was a local eyesore of shabby souvenir shops, cheap restaurants and public houses. Most premises were relics of the days when the majority of visitors arrived by sea on the London paddle steamers.

The Fort Road improvement scheme of 1938 to 1946 changed the whole neighbourhood. The council compulsorily purchased seventy-seven properties, including thirty-seven shops, two hotels and fifteen cottages. All were swept away when the present dual carriageway was constructed, opening up the wide panoramic view of the bay.

Princes Walk & Foreness Point, Margate.

At the east of the town, Cliftonville is almost merging with neighbouring Kingsgate. The Princes Walk on the top of the cliffs was opened by the then Prince of Wales in 1926. This gave an impetus to housing development inland, and the later construction of the concrete promenade not only prevented cliff erosion but was another attraction for visitors enjoying quieter beaches.

FORENESS POINT AND BAY, CLIFTONVILLE.

Hazardous Row was the original name of Albert Terrace. The High Street shops shown here in an early nineteenth-century print were built on the low chalk cliffs with little protection from the pounding of the sea. The great January storm of 1808 destroyed this whole area.

Land reclamation and the construction of the Marine Drive and promenades meant that the frontage was set back and the attractive Marine Gardens with seating and flower beds was developed.

Cecil Square has always been the centre of Margate's municipal activities since first being laid out in 1769. This shows a 1902 photograph of a rally of some of Margate's early motor cars. The corner site is taken up by the Grand Theatre, later to be renamed the Hippodrome. Cecil Square is now a busy centre for the most of town's bus routes and taxi ranks. In 1970 the Hippodrome and the adjoining buildings were demolished to make way for the present library, council chamber and municipal offices.

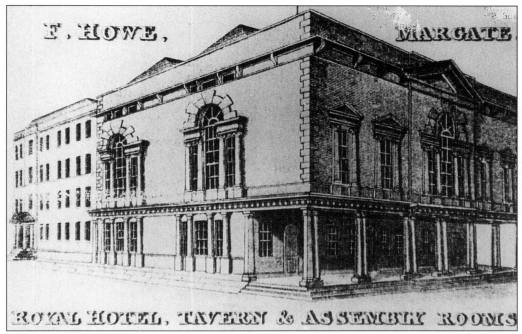

The Royal Hotel and Assembly Rooms on the corner of Cecil Square were the centre of royal and aristocratic patronage in Margate's early days, when the fishing village around the harbour was merging into the farming community around St John's church. The Royal Hotel was renamed in 1794 when the Prince of Wales (later King George IV) first met Caroline of Brunswick in the hotel before his disastrous arranged marriage.

This corner is now occupied by the library and the municipal offices of Thanet District Council.

Cranbourne Alley was a narrow passageway of small shops and second hand stores which linked the commercial area of the town with the parish church of St John's.

With increasing private car ownership it was necessary to demolish several blocks of Old Margate in 1952. This enabled the road-widening scheme which allowed easier access into the town centre.

In every town shopping patterns have changed through the years. The Town Market, behind the old Town Hall, had licences in 1821 for forty-three stalls, mainly fish, fruit and vegetables. In 1897 the municipal offices were built on the site, and the number of stalls was reduced and trade declined.

Today the Market Place exists in name only. One family with a fruit and vegetable stall traded here from 1919, but closed down in 1982. A small coffee stall is all that remains.

As Margate expanded eastwards into Cliftonville, the first terrace in Northdown Road was the twelve gable ends of Magdala Villas. They commanded a fine view inland over the wooded Dane, later to be developed as Dane Park. The other direction allowed an uninterrupted view of the sea and shipping over the cliff-top fields.

Today Northdown Road is a thriving shopping street, with ten of the original gable ends still recognizable. The ground floors of what were prestigious residences have now been converted into busy shops.

MARGATE ROAD, BIRCHINGTON-ON-SEA.

When most visitors arrived in Margate by either sea or rail, the roads into the town were often narrow with no pavements. At the turn of the century, pedestrians often had to walk along dirt tracks avoiding the horse traffic.

Margate Road, Birchington, now carries constant car and coach traffic during the summer months. The road is now skirted with houses and bungalows, an unbroken ribbon development of several miles.

The Parade and Lower High Street were visitors' first sight of Margate when most of them arrived by sea. With the coming of the railways in 1846 and 1863, it was important to link the harbour area with newly developing Westbrook, and so Marine Drive was constructed in 1880. The bow-windowed Ingoldsby House is where Barham wrote the Ingoldsby legends.

Ingoldsby House is now a gentlemen's outfitters, but the rest of the frontage has been redeveloped with European funding. Garner's Library became the Imperial Hotel in 1880. In 1996 the Imperial was refurbished into a night club with penthouse suites.

Two
The Influence of the Sea

The sea has been an enemy to Margate as well as a friend.

Margate is recorded as our earliest seaside resort in 1736 when a channel was cut from the site of this tavern. Salt water would enter at every tide, and thus a commercial bath was opened. Bathing and drinking salt water were advocated as a panacea for many medical conditions.

This corner site on the Parade was converted into the residential Royal York Mansions in 1909. It later reverted into the present licensed premises, the Ruby Lounge. The original channel disappeared when the Parade was widened in 1868, using land reclaimed from the harbour area.

Margate jetty was opened in 1855, replacing the original wooden structure of 1824. Before the railways and the popularity of motor transport, all visitors to Margate would arrive by sea. When the last steamer sailed from here in 1956, the jetty was already in decline as essential maintenance became too expensive to be commercially viable.

The present scene is a sad-looking memorial of twisted iron girders, all that remains after the great winter storm of 1978, when the whole superstructure was battered, breached and finally swept away. Heavy seas each succeeding winter see a little more swept away.

The early Margate seaside resort was centred on the bathing rooms in the Lower High Street. They were the social centres for the visitors of the day, who then went out for the salt water cure in the hooded bathing machines. Coffees, sherbet and jellies would be consumed, newspapers would be read and impromptu musical recitals given. The great winter storm of 1808 ravaged and swept away most of the Lower High Street. Later, most of the bathing rooms were rebuilt, but they never regained their former popularity, as they now faced competition from other forms of relaxation and entertainment.

Today, the site of the original Bathing Rooms is occupied by single storey shops. Despite commercial pressures, the shops remain single storey. Building covenants still protect the sea views of the former residential premises opposite, despite Marine Drive being built in front in 1880. Today's busy High Street is thus still able to evoke a visual memory of Margate's early bathing history.

Another casualty of winter storms and lack of maintenance was the Westbrook Pavilion, the summer home of variety stars and the big bands between the wars. Built in 1910, it replaced a wooden bandstand. Wartime evacuation and damage by stray floating mines hastened its end, which finally came with the damage caused by the winter storms of 1953.

It remained an open site until the present 'Leisure Time' children's amusement centre and café was opened on this promenade site in the 1980s.

This section deals with damage suffered by Margate through the winter storms. A striking picture comes from 1978 when the wooden decking from the jetty, a mile away, washed up on the sands of Marine Terrace. Earlier, a grand piano from a storm which destroyed the Marine Palace was washed up in Palm Bay some two miles away.

The same section of sands on a peaceful summer's day. Holiday makers and deck chairs stand in place of the storm-tossed wooden planking.

The soft chalk cliffs of Margate and Cliftonville have always been susceptible to coastal erosion by the ravages of the sea and concrete promenades have had to be built to protect the town's nine miles of coastline.

The Fort and Lower Promenade, Cliftonville

The cliffs shown here were excavated to form the foundations for the concrete promenades in 1911. The great amphitheatre left by the excavations was then converted into the resort asset of the Winter Gardens.

Winter storms also caused the disappearance of Pettman's Bathing Platform in Cliftonville. For seventy-five years, until the 1939 war, the mile-long platform at the base of the cliffs provided bathing facilities described as 'being distinctly select and decidedly superior to any others on the coast'. The Pettman family operated over 100 machines and cabins.

Maintenance costs were always a problem, and the bathing platform was never rebuilt after the decaying effects of six years of evacuation and war in 1945. Today a new promenade has been constructed on the site.

The regularity of winter storms on this coast was responsible for the re-siting of the Royal Navy Air Station in St. Mildred's Bay in 1916. This card shows the hangar and radio mast of the seaplane station in the First World War. The hangar was blown into the sea and several seaplanes were destroyed in March 1916. This resulted in the air base being moved two miles inland to establish RAF Manston, later to become Kent International Airport.

Some eighty years later the coastline and garden walks are little changed. The buildings to the right are noteworthy as being on the site of the first 'bengalo', or bungalow, in England in 1867.

Three
Changes in Holiday Activities

The Promenade and Ethelbert Terrace, Cliftonville.

Then, visitors spent far more time strolling along the promenades. Now, modern visitors to Margate seem far less energetic.

The pattern of bathing has changed considerably since the war. Most bathers used to be happy in open air bathing pools fed by the cool waters of the sea. The main bathing pool shown here was opened in 1926, backed by a whole complex, including a theatre, dance hall, arcades, and at least six restaurants and bars.

The pool today is a sad sight. It finally closed down in 1957, when swimming fashions changed and the majority of visitors preferred the heated indoor pool of the Hartsdown Leisure Centre.

Also in 1926, the Sun Deck Bathing Pavilion was built near the Lifeboatman Memorial to provide bathing cabins and facilities for the western end of Marine Terrace sands.

An outdoor pool was opened here in 1937 when free bathing from the sands was prohibited. Expensive maintenance and a change in swimming habits caused the Sun Deck to be demolished in 1990. A beneficial effect of this was to open up several miles of golden sands westwards at low tide.

In the past, Margate relied on its visitors staying in boarding and guest houses for a fortnight's 'bucket and spade' break. At peak times hardly a space would be visible on the golden sands, a magnet for a mix of pulsating humanity, buckets and spades, cold ice cream and warm beer.

In company with other similar seaside resorts, the sands are often less crowded now as visitors appear to stay for shorter periods. Ownership of private cars and the growth in group coach parties mean that more people now use the town as a base for touring the area. The sands now face the occasionally windswept foreshore.

A noticeable change is evident in the 'Golden Mile' of Marine Terrace. This pre-war photograph shows a line of shops selling Margate rock, postcards and souvenirs, interspersed with ice cream stalls, fish and chip shops and gypsy fortune tellers.

Today the frontage is taken over by an unbroken line of neon-lit amusement arcades, with their flashing electronic games and strident amplification of music and sound. Modern visitors no longer feel it is essential to take home a stick of Margate rock.

Another social change is the decline in formal dining. Evening dress was essential for dining in the Queen's Highcliffe Hotel between the wars. Lavish facilities and impeccable behaviour were the keynotes, and dinner menus would often feature eight separate courses.

When Butlin's took over the Queen's Highcliffe and five other Cliftonville hotels between 1955 and 1957, holiday breaks for a mass market took over. All-in prices meant communal dining in an informal atmosphere. Redcoats provided activities and entertainment to relieve any holiday boredom.

The G.S.N. Co.'s "GOLDEN EAGLE,"
LONDON, MARGATE, RAMSGATE, BOULOGNE, &c.

Visitors today no longer thrill to the excitement of boarding the Margate steamers for trips to France. Now it is so much more convenient to cross the Channel on day trips from Ramsgate or Dover, or use Le Shuttle through the Channel Tunnel.

No longer do the crowded pleasure boats, like the Moss Rose shown here, leave Margate Harbour for trips out to sea. It was a memorable experience for so many visitors in the past, despite mops for seasickness being an essential part of the ship's inventory.

Cricket on the Sands, Cliftonville.

This page and the page opposite show holiday activities for which there are no contemporary comparisons. No more does one see the sporting competitions between the various guest houses and boarding houses. Often the same people would visit the same establishment in the same week each year. Everyone seemed to know each other.

Keep fit classes on the sands are also no more. Pre-war reports describe some Keep fit classes on the sands as being 'over 200 strong'. Today's visitors go to the indoor classes in the Leisure Centre.

Sandcastle competitions have also disappeared. National newspapers would offer considerable monetary prizes, often won by adults who were young at heart with their children looking on. Large areas of Marine Sands would be roped off on a certain day each week.

Between the wars the sands would offer a great variety of activities. There would be bathing from the machines where there was segregation between the sexes, donkey rides, pierrots, concert parties, Punch and Judy, beach photographers, religious mission services, and dozens of itinerant hawkers of ice cream, drinks and fruit.

A postcard of fifty years ago shows that long promenade walks along the top of the cliffs were a popular form of exercise. They would often finish up at tea gardens and restaurants such as the Koh-i-Noor, later the Bungalow Restaurant.

Increasing dependence on cars meant less walking, and this site is now derelict. A fire in 1975 caused considerable damage and the building was never rebuilt. Increasing dependence on cars meant less walking and this site is now derelict. A fire in 1975 caused considerable damage and the building was never rebuilt. Unfortunately, ambitious plans for a Seacology Centre here have now been abandoned despite the site's clearance as shown here.

The boating pool near the harbour was a magnet for children before the war. Queues would often form for the fleet of hand-driven paddle boats, and crowds of children would paddle in the shallow end.

Like the harbour in the background, the pool has silted up over the years. More sand and less water become evident every year.

Dreamland Amusement Park has always been a popular attraction for day trippers and staying visitors alike. When it opened in 1919 it featured simple rides and amusements with a fairground atmosphere of coconut stalls and raffle prizes. The greatest thrill was the Scenic Railway.

Today's visitors now demand more and more thrills with the various 'white knuckle' rides. The great wheel shown here is one of the largest in the country, and has recently been redeveloped.

Four
Holiday
Accommodation
and Fashion

Before the war there was a complete absence of casual clothing on holiday. Hats, coats, collars, ties and even plus fours were the norm.

Margate's working-class visitors often preferred the less structured atmosphere of the local boarding houses as a cheap informal alternative to guest houses and private hotels. This shows a 1925 group outside Luton House, in the Victorian terrace of Union Crescent.

Today, the same premises have deteriorated into multiple occupancy flats. Although planning regulations are tighter, absentee landlords often disregard essential maintenance, as shown by the peeling paint work and shabby façades.

Queens Highcliffe Hotel. Cliftonville.

At the turn of the century Margate and Cliftonville had many luxury hotels, such as the Queen's Highcliffe Hotel. They were open all year round, had permanent orchestras, hairdressing salons and accommodation for accompanying servants and nannies.

Two world wars and attendant social upheavals meant facilities were increasingly being provided for a decreasing clientele. In 1955 Butlin's took over, but two disastrous fires in 1974 meant almost complete demolition. Many redevelopment schemes were proposed and rejected. Finally in 1993 the present Queens Court complex of 126 housing units was completed.

Another purpose-built hotel was the Cliftonville Hotel, built in 1868 on an open site surrounded by cornfields. It catered for wealthy visitors who often brought down their own servants and carriages. The hotel had its Palm Court Orchestra and in 1906 it was stated that 'Lords and Ladies visiting here might fancy themselves at Cannes'.

After six years of wartime desolation, this imposing monument to a past age was in decline, through inadequate maintenance, increasing costs and changing clientele. By 1956 it had been demolished, and in February 1963 a bowling alley, with adjoining night club and restaurant, was opened on the site.

Parading the latest fashions was important. Guide books between the wars would recommend that ladies staying in Cliftonville hotels should pack at least forty dresses and a dozen hats for their stay. This shows the Queen's Promenade after church attendance on a Sunday in August 1919.

Today's photograph is of the same scene on a Sunday in August. Contemporary visitors no longer parade in their finery, but prefer more active pursuits.

Seventy-five years separate these two photographs on the seafront at Margate. In the past, visitors would often wear the same clothing as they wore at home and at work. A trilby hat, a bowler or a flat cap would indicate subtle class distinctions. Collars and ties would be the norm, even on the beach. Today, casual clothing is universal. A collar and tie would seem out of place, and holiday clothing no longer shows a distinction in class or occupation.

When most of Margate's visitors arrived by sea, the main hotels were around the harbour area. This shows the White Hart Hotel on the Parade, an establishment dating back to 1717. For most of the nineteenth century this was Margate's leading hotel. Both Gladstone and Disraeli featured in the visitors' book.

As with several other Margate hotels, it did not modernize to meet the requirements of modern visitors. After a period of declining fortunes it was demolished in 1967. Today the site is occupied by the White Hart Mansions block, a conversion into flats with attractive views over the sea.

Another demolished hotel is the Hotel Metropole facing the entrance to the jetty. Originally Turner painted some of his watercolours from the Foy Boat Inn near this site. A fire later destroyed the Grand Hotel which was replaced by the 100-room Hotel Metropole in 1893. With the decline in arrivals by sea between the wars, the hotel struggled to retain its custom.

The end came with the Fort Road improvement scheme between 1938 and 1946 when the dual carriageway was constructed opening up the panoramic view of the town from Fort Hill.

One noticeable change in fashion between then and now is in bathing costumes. The two piece bikini costume for ladies and swimming trunks for men came into fashion after the Second World War. There was little personal ownership of swimming costumes and most were hired from the bathing establishments. They were standard fashion in navy blue, covering the whole body to just above the knees. Bathing caps were considered essential for the ladies.

Even when going down to the beach, there was a general uniformity of clothing seventy-five years ago. It was rare to see an open-necked shirt, and neither gentlemen nor ladies would forego their headgear. Male visitors to Margate were fond of their flat cloth caps, while trilbies and bowlers were more suitable for Cliftonville.

Five

Entertainment
and Transport

Margate Minstrels, providing simple and unsophisticated entertainment.

At one time Margate boasted five open-air bandstands where military bands and concert parties attracted large audiences. This scene in 1950 at the Oval Bandstand shows their popularity continued after the war. Many well known entertainers learnt their trade before audiences such as these.

Over recent years open air shows have lost their popularity due to the unpredictability of the English summer. The Oval Bandstand has hosted local groups and wrestling competitions and has sometimes been threatened with closure, but has now been taken over by the Cliftonville Residents Association.

Until 1939 concert parties on Marine Terrace Sands attracted packed audiences. Originally the minstrels were here, followed by the pierrots and Harry Gold's concert parties. Their popularity waned as modern audiences no longer related to the simple humour and unsophisticated sketches of pre-amplification days.

Today the concert party stage site has been taken over by bouncy castles, trampolining and fairground-type children's swings.

The age of the seaside cinema was between the wars. The original Hall by the Sea became the Dreamland Hall in 1919. Until 1935 the cinema here always had a small orchestra backing two variety acts during the interval.

In 1936 the Dreamland Cinema was rebuilt, becoming the tall focal point of Margate's brash sea frontage. Recent changes in cinema-going habits have converted the original 2000-seat cinema into smaller centres.

The first bandstand in Margate was on the Fort Green, the home for visiting military bands and the Town Band. In 1911 the site was converted into a vast amphitheatre, dug out by pick and shovel; the soil was removed by horse and cart to provide foundations for promenades.

The great hollow which was left became the Winter Gardens, a great summer asset to the resort. In its time it has played host to national conferences, summer shows, pop and symphony concerts, and balls and banquets for civic functions.

One of the earliest provincial theatres is Margate's Theatre Royal built in 1786, when the town was developing into a leading resort. It was regularly patronized by royalty and the aristocracy.

For more than 200 years the theatre has had a chequered existence, beset by only being commercially viable for a few summer months. The future is now much brighter with an enthusiastic group of friends aided by lottery funding taking the theatre into the new century.

Another Margate theatre was the New Grand Theatre, opened in 1898 on the corner of Cecil Square. The name was changed to the Hippodrome in 1905, when touring West End musical comedies and Edwardian music hall were staged here. Through the years the theatre was used for repertory and variety shows, as well as being a cinema.

It finally closed in 1957. The buildings were demolished and in 1971 a new Magistrates' Court was opened. This was followed in 1974 by the Margate public library and municipal offices.

There has been a marked change in the transport by which visitors arrive in the town. For nearly a century, thousands of holidaymakers would stream off the London paddle steamers from the jetty. The scene by the Droit House would always be lively and crowded, as this was the centre for horse brakes, coaches and trams to all parts of Thanet.

Nowadays, this harbour area is quiet even in the summer months, as the great majority of visitors now arrive by private car, motor coaches or by rail.

An early hovercraft service operated from Marine Sands in 1966. This only operated for a short period as the Pier Company invoked an 1812 Act claiming a levy for every passenger. It was also felt that the noise 'would upset the donkeys'. The service then moved to Ramsgate Harbour and then to the Pegwell Bay Hoverport when it opened in May 1969. Now hovercraft services operate from Dover and Folkestone, and Margate Sands are left in peace.

Before the development of motor transport most visitors would enjoy trips by horse brakes to the local tea gardens, to Canterbury and to historical sites in East Kent. This card shows Tanting's team of greys outside the Nayland Rock Hotel in September 1910.

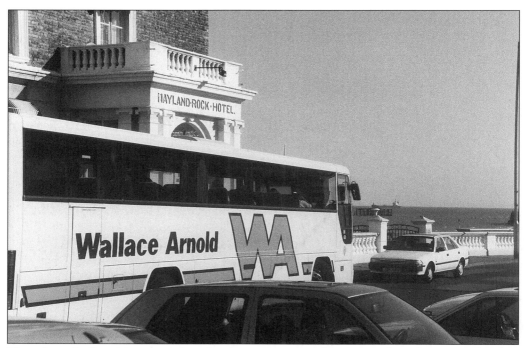

Nowadays, similar visits are made either by private car or by organized coach parties. Coaches and cars still park outside the Nayland Rock Hotel in place of the horse brakes.

Horse brakes lining up on Marine Drive for day trips to neighbouring parts of East Kent. The background shows Marine Terrace as attractive apartment houses. Today the ground floors have been converted into amusement arcades.

Another form of transport which has disappeared is the solid-tyred charabanc. These took over from the horse brakes, but at least had a folded roof for the wet weather. Each row of seats was entered separately, but the solid tyres gave rather a bumpy ride.

The first railway came to Margate via Ramsgate in 1846, and the first station was opened on Marine Terrace seafront. This was Margate Sands Station which closed in 1926, when Margate West became the main station on its present site.

The Margate Sands Station site is now occupied by gift shops and the Arlington arcade.

The tramway system opened in 1899 and linked Margate, Broadstairs and Ramsgate. They provided a useful link around the island. During the season they would run from half past five in the morning until midnight. The last tram ran in 1936.

The transport links in Margate some seventy-five years ago. The visitors would arrive by the steam boats, and then had the choice of horse brakes, carriages or trams to take them to their accommodation.

In the past, most Margate shopkeepers had their own small delivery vans, which until the First World War were generally horse drawn. A.H. Bowkett, the local baker, would deliver to boarding houses and hotels on a daily basis. With private car ownership and large car parks at the supermarkets this facility is no longer required except for very heavy loads.

Six

Shops and Changes
in Function

Many buildings alter with social and
economic change. The Fountain Inn
in Fort Road, old established
licensed premises, is now Lloyds
Bank.

Commercial changes have reshaped the physical shape of town streets. The small individual shops in Queen Street have now given way to the pedestrianized shopping arcade 'The Centre'. The multiple stores with their well known names have taken over from Margate family businesses such as V.J. Woolls, Thornton Bobby and Tully and Markey.

Station Road, Birchington - on - Sea.

As the population increased and Margate expanded east and west, once residential roads became shopping streets. In 1907 Station Road, Birchington, was residential with just two shops. Today it is the main shopping street in the area.

BOBBY & CO.'S CLIFTONVILLE ENTERPRISE.

SOME DETAILS OF THE SPLENDIDLY EQUIPPED PREMISES OPENED TO-DAY.

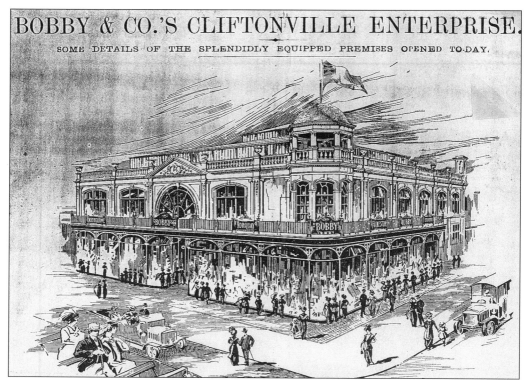

Bobby's purpose built department store opened in Northdown Road in June 1913. Tea dances in the Palm Court Restaurant were held with orchestra and vocalists until 1939. Morning coffee and afternoon teas were revived in 1950, but never regained their former popularity. With ease of car ownership and the expansion of department stores in nearby Canterbury, Margate's only department store closed in January 1973 and the whole block was converted into individual shops.

Possibly the greatest change in shopping habits is the popularity of supermarkets. The College supermarket is on the site of Margate College, which was an oasis of trees and green lawns near Cecil Square. Margate College was a minor public school established in 1886 to 'train leaders of men to govern our Empire'. It suffered war damage in September 1941 and was never rebuilt. After many years as an improvised car park it was developed as a supermarket site in 1987.

The Victorian Prospect Tavern is also the site for a supermarket store opened in 1997. This tavern with its bowling green was a popular venue in Zion Place for Margate's early visitors. It linked the developing area of Cliftonville with the original seaside settlement around Margate Harbour.

The Kent Hotel and public house was a Marine Terrace feature for over a hundred years. A typical uninhibited Victorian pub, it was popular with the Cockney day trippers and works outings between the wars.

In 1987 this corner became the Flamingo amusement arcade and well illustrates the social change from convivial drinks to the instant fun induced by the flashing and bleeping electronic games machines.

Another change in function is the Royal Sea Bathing Hospital on Canterbury Road. Founded in 1791, it was the country's first specialized hospital compared to the normal general hospitals. It advocated salt water bathing and the benefits of bracing sea air in cases of consumption.

After 200 years, NHS policy favoured the expansion of the General Hospital in Margate. The building is now up for sale, but due to its condition and partial listed building status, it is difficult to incorporate an alternative use.

Shaftesbury House on Marine
Gardens is another example of
Victorian philanthropic grandeur
which has outgrown its use. In
1887 the building was presented
to the YMCA for use as a seaside
home. In 1919 Dr Barnardo's took
over the premises for orphan
children from the East End.

Later the buildings became a poor quality
amusement arcade, with cheap souvenir shops.
In 1988 the top three floors were destroyed by
fire. It has now been rebuilt to provide self-
contained flats with attractive views over the
sea.

Between 1870 and 1920 there were forty-eight orphanages and convalescent homes listed in the local directories. The West Ham Convalescent Home in Northdown Road was originally built in 1882 as a home 'for illegitimate fatherless boys under twelve to take advantage of open air bathing and healthy, bracing sea breezes'.

With the introduction of the NHS in 1948, the need for such buildings declined. The whole surrounding area of Zion Place was compulsorily purchased, and the site is now a petrol station. Northumberland Hall to the right still retains its original façade.

Another corner which changed its function is in Hawley Square. This was Bettison's circulating library much patronized by 'officers and gentry of rank and fashion' in the early nineteenth century. The library opened in 1786 and remained there for fifty-seven years. It was an important social meeting place for Margate's early visitors with card playing, musical evenings and raffles.

Today the corner site is occupied by the Hilderstone Adult Education Centre, opened in the 1960s, which took over the Thanet School of Art building opened in 1931. It is a striking example of 1930s architecture.

An enemy air raid on 1 June 1943 destroyed Holy Trinity church which had looked benevolently over Margate since it was built in 1826. As Margate extended into Cliftonville, there was no church provision to the east.

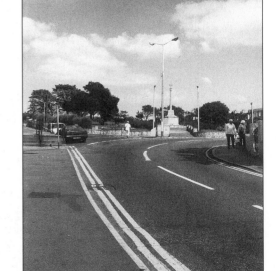

The War Memorial and the gardens still remain. The site of this former striking landmark was finally cleared in 1959, and is now one of the town's car parks.

The two old fishermen's cottages shown here once occupied a corner of King Street. Built in 1683, they fell into disrepair and by 1936 were judged as unfit for human habitation. In a poor state of repair and damaged by wartime action, they were restored in 1951 as an example of Tudor architecture, using some of the beams and plasterwork from the original cottages. The local Tudor House Committee handed the premises over to the local authority in 1958 to be used as a Museum.

The site of one of the oldest shop premises in Margate is on the corner of High Street with Queen Street. John Bayly's tea dealership and cheesemonger's shop had a sign 'established 1697' when it was rebuilt in 1860. The High Street was then known as the King's Highway, and as late as 1881 there was no drainage or sewers. Until 1890 all water came from the wells to the rear.

This section of the High Street was redeveloped in 1971, when the corner shops disappeared and the chain stores came in. It is now pedestrianized and part of The Centre shopping complex.

J.M.W. Turner, the great watercolour artist, had a close association with Margate. This shows the lodging house on Bankside near the jetty, where he lodged with Mrs Sophia Booth for many years in the first half of the nineteenth century.

This whole area has now been demolished and redeveloped. Turner's association with Margate is commemorated by the historic blue plaque on the wall of the Ship Inn. This approximates to the location of Mrs Booth's house.

Hoopers Hill House on Northdown Road was named after Hooper's Mill, an unusual windmill with horizontal sweeps built in 1770. The original house was built by Sir Thomas Cavaler at the same time. He was reputed to have 'the finest wine cellars in the whole of Kent'. The house was demolished in 1960, but it is interesting that the site is now occupied by a tourist attraction known as Margate Caves or the Vortigern Caves. Could it be that these caves, a source of considerable local folklore and historical inaccuracies, have been converted from the old wine cellars?

Seven
Miscellany

This card posted in Margate in 1905 illustrates the characters to be seen on an Edwardian seaside holiday in the town.

The lack of political correctness is noticeable in many seaside scenes from Margate's past. Often in the side shows at the Dreamland Amusement Park, midget troupes, deformed characters and performing animals would be exploited. This card shows the Royal Coronation Midgets featured at Dreamland in 1937.

White-skinned minstrels would appear with cork-blackened faces. A popular show on Marine Terrace Sands was the 'Dandy Coons' concert party.

Until 1956 the London steamers would bring in visitors to the jetty in their thousands. The Bandstand was always crowded and in the concert pavilion there was generally a concert party and ladies' orchestra. Now only the rusting girders which supported the jetty extension remain as a sad nostalgic memory.

Jetty, Margate (Showing Fleet)

Another sight never to return are the battleships and cruisers of the Royal Navy fleet anchored offshore on recruiting drives during the summer months. The naval base at Chatham was only forty miles away.

No miscellany of Then and Now scenes in Margate would be complete without showing the revolution in the school classrooms. A classroom in Holy Trinity School in 1938 shows straight-backed children, the desks in straight rows, hard wooden seats, and inkwells which were regularly filled by the ink monitors.

Today there is a greater informality in the classroom, now well stocked with computers to bring the younger generation into the age of information technology.

Two more Margate photographs showing scenes long forgotten. The playground in St. John's school just after the First World War shows a regimented PE class of the period. Most schools did not have gymnasiums and there would be fifty or more children in a class. Even while exercising, the boys did not remove their hard starched collars.

Uncle Frank was a regular on Margate sea front in 1935. Reputed to be England's heaviest man, you only paid him if he guessed your weight correctly.

Fashions in music and dance have also changed. Between the wars the Louis Seize Ballroom in the Queen's Highcliffe Hotel would be crowded with residents in ball gowns and evening dress, dancing to the permanent resident orchestra of between ten and twelve musicians.

The Butlin's organisation purchased the Queen's Highcliffe and the St George's Hotels in 1957. Dances became much more informal with the popularity of pop music. The large bands of the past were reduced to just two musicians, and then later to a disco with a DJ.

Sports activities have also changed. Before the war croquet lawns were available on St George's Lawns. Before television, large hoardings were erected here and visitors could follow cricket test matches ball by ball through the early radio broadcasts.

Today, the St George's Lawns are more popular bowls centres, with thriving local clubs staging national competitions.

OLD MARGATE

A tidal inlet called the Creek flowed through Dane Valley into the harbour. By the nineteenth century it had deteriorated into a mini-sewer and a dump for household refuse. A wooden bridge was built across to allow contact between the Parade and the Fort.

The bridge was later taken down, and the waters of the Creek were incorporated into the drainage system of the town. This allowed the Parade to be widened, and King Street then became a more important thoroughfare.

Dent-de-Lion Gateway,
Garlinge, Margate.

A fine fortified gateway is all that remains of the fifteenth century mansion at Dent de Lion. In the early days of seaside holidays Dent de Lion became an exclusive tavern and coffee house, with bowling green and archery grounds. In1888 a fire destroyed the mansion and all the farm buildings, leaving only the ancient gateway with its well prison under the tower.

An attractive redevelopment of the estate in 1982 incorporated the gateway into high quality housing.

Gloucester Lodge was opposite Hoopers Hill House in Northdown Road. It was the early nineteenth-century home of Dr David Price, a local doctor and surgeon. All the windows at the front were later filled in. In the days before detailed anatomical knowledge was available, surgeons often had to obtain dead bodies from hospitals and churchyards. Local legend spread rumours that Ben Crouch, a notorious seller of dead bodies who lived locally in the Crown and Anchor in Zion Place, sold bodies to Dr Price.

In 1960 Gloucester Lodge was demolished together with the flint-walled houses of Flint Row. Today the site is occupied by pleasant corporation flatlets.